on

LOVE

on LOVE

POPE FRANCIS

LOYOLAPRESS.
A JESUIT MINISTRY
Chicago

LOYOLA PRESS.
A JESUIT MINISTRY

3441 N. Ashland Avenue
Chicago, Illinois 60657
(800) 621-1008
www.loyolapress.com

Cover art credit: ROMAOSLO/iStock/Getty Images

ISBN: 978-0-8294-4867-2
Library of Congress Control Number: 2019951770

Printed in the United States of America.
19 20 21 22 23 24 25 26 27 28 Bang 10 9 8 7 6 5 4 3 2 1

Contents

Contents

Contents

CONTENTS

1

Love Is Kindled in Darkness

At times, the dark of night seems to penetrate the soul. At times, we think, "There is nothing more to be done," and the heart no longer finds the strength to love. . . . But it is precisely in this darkness that Christ lights the fire of God's love: a flash breaks through and announces a new start—something begins in the deepest darkness. We know that the night is "most night-like" just before the dawn. In that very darkness, Christ conquers and rekindles the fire of love.

2

God's Love Never Ends

There will never be a day in our lives in which we cease to be a concern for the heart of God. God is always concerned about us, and he walks with us. Why does he do this? Because he loves us. Is this understood? He loves us! And God will surely provide for all our needs. He will not abandon us in times of trial and darkness. This certainty seeks to settle in our souls and never be extinguished.

3

God's Love Waits for Us

The mystery of God's love is not revealed to the wise and the intelligent but to the little ones (Luke 10:21; Matthew 11:25–26). Therefore, the most profound lesson we are called to transmit—and the most certain way to get out of doubt—is to embrace the love of God, which we have always had (1 John 4:10). A great love, free and given to us forever. God never goes back on his love! He always moves forward and waits.

Let us remember this in our lives as Christians: Even when we have left him behind, God waits for us. He is never far from us, and, if we return to him, he is ready to embrace us.

4
Rock-Solid Love

The love of God is stable and secure, like the rocky shores that provide shelter from the violence of the waves. Jesus manifests this [love] in the miracle recounted in the Gospel, when he calms the storm, commanding the wind and the sea (Mark 4:41). The disciples are afraid because they realize that they may not survive the storm, but Jesus opens their hearts to the courage of faith. To the man who cries out, "I can't do it anymore," the Lord . . . offers the rock of his love, to which everyone can cling, assured of not falling. How many times do we feel that we can't do it anymore? But He is near us, with his outstretched hand and open heart.

5

Generous Love

The Lord proclaims himself to be "abounding in steadfast love and faithfulness." How beautiful this definition of God is! It is all-encompassing. God is great and powerful, and this greatness and power are used to love us, who are so small, so incompetent. The word "love" connotes *affection, grace, goodness*. God's love is not soap-opera love. It is love that takes the first step, love that does not depend on human merit but on immense generosity. Nothing can stop this generosity, not even sin, because God's love transcends sin, overcomes evil, and forgives it.

6

God's Love Is Tangible

God is not some vague entity like a mist. . . . He is tangible and has a name: "God is love." His is not a sentimental, emotional kind of love but the love of the Father who is the origin of all life, the love of the Son who dies on the Cross and is raised, and the love of the Spirit who renews human beings and the world. Thinking that God is love does us so much good because it teaches us to love, it teaches us to give ourselves to others as Jesus gave himself to us and walks with us. Jesus walks beside us on the road through life.

7

God's Love Is Close to Us

We are all called to witness and proclaim the message that "God is love." God isn't far from or insensitive to our human affairs. He is close to us, always beside us, walking with us to share our joys and our sorrows, our hopes and our struggles. He loves us very much, and for that reason, he became human. He came into the world not to condemn it but so the world would be saved through Jesus (John 3:16–17). And this is the love of God in Jesus, this love that is so difficult to understand but that we feel when we draw close to Jesus. Jesus always forgives us, always awaits us; he loves us so much. We can feel the love of Jesus and the love of God.

8

God's Love Transforms

The love of God re-creates everything—that is, God makes all things new. When we recognize our limits and our weaknesses, we open the door to the forgiveness of Jesus, to a love that can deeply renew us, that can re-create us. Salvation can enter our hearts when we allow ourselves to experience the truth and recognize our mistakes and our sins. Now let us create that beautiful experience of [the one] who has come not for the healthy but for the sick, not for the just ones but for the sinners (Matthew 9:12–13). Let us experience his patience, his tenderness, and his will to save all.

9

The Ultimate Sign of Love

Isaiah's prophecy announces the rising of a great light that breaks through the night. This light is born in Bethlehem and is welcomed by the loving arms of Mary, by the love of Joseph, and by the wonder of the shepherds. When the angels announced the birth of the Redeemer to the shepherds, they did so with these words: "This will be a sign for you: you will find a baby wrapped in swaddling clothes and lying in a manger" (Luke 2:12).

The sign is in fact the humility of God . . . taken to the extreme. It is the love with which, that night, God assumed our frailty, our suffering, our anxieties, our desires, and our limitations. The message that everyone was expecting, that everyone was searching for in the depths of their souls, was none other than the tenderness of God—God who looks upon us with eyes full of love, who accepts our poverty, who is in love with our smallness.

10

Love Carries Us through Uncertainty

By decree of the Emperor, Mary and Joseph found themselves forced to leave their people, their home, and their land, and undertake a journey to be registered in the census. This was no comfortable or easy journey for a young couple who were about to have a child. At heart, they were full of hope and expectation because of the child about to be born. Yet their steps were weighed down by the uncertainties and dangers that follow those who must leave home behind.

And there [in Bethlehem], where everything was a challenge, Mary gave us Emmanuel. The Son of God had to be born in a stable because his own people had no room for him. "He came to what was his own and his own people did not accept him" (John 1:11). Amid the gloom of a city that had no room for the stranger from afar, amid the darkness of this bustling city, the revolutionary spark of God's love was kindled. In Bethlehem, a door opens for those who have lost their land, their country, their dreams, for those who are overcome with suffering from a life of isolation.

11

The Bread of Love

Christmas, above all, has a taste of hope because, for all the darkness in our lives, God's light shines forth. His gentle light does not frighten us. By being born poor and frail in our midst, God becomes one of us and draws us to himself with tenderness. He is born in Bethlehem, which means "house of bread." In this way, God seems to tell us that he is born as bread for us. He enters our life to give us his life; he comes into our world to give us his love.

He does not come to lord this love over us but to feed and serve us. There is a straight line between the manger and the cross where Jesus will become *bread that is broken*. It is the straight line of love that gives and saves, the love that brings light to our lives and peace to our hearts.

12

Loving the Child Jesus

The Child Jesus comes to save us. He comes to show us the face of the Father who is abounding in love and mercy. Therefore, let us hold the Child Jesus tightly in our arms; let us place ourselves at his service.

It is important that we place Jesus at the center of our lives and know, even if it may seem paradoxical, that it is our responsibility to protect him. The Child Jesus wants to be in our embrace, he wants to be tended to and to be able to gaze upon us. Additionally, we must make the Child Jesus smile in order to show him our love and our joy that he is in our midst. His smile is a sign of the love that gives us the assurance of being loved.

13
God's Love Is Humble

The star that led the wise men on the journey allowed them to enter the mystery. Led by the Spirit, they came to realize that God's criteria were quite different from people's: God does not manifest himself in the power of this world but speaks to us in the humbleness of his love. God's love is great. God's love is powerful. But the love of God is humble. The wise men are thus models of conversion to the true faith because they believed more in the goodness of God than in the apparent splendor of power.

14
God's Power Is Love

Christ's word is powerful: it doesn't have the world's power but God's, which is strong in humility and in weakness. His power is that of love—a love that knows no boundaries, a love that lets us love others before ourselves. The word of Jesus, the holy Gospel, teaches that the truly blessed are poor in spirit, non-violent, meek, workers of peace and justice. This is the word that gives strength and is capable of changing the world. There is no other way to change the world.

15

Love Incarnate

The grace that was revealed to our world is Jesus, born of the Virgin Mary, true man and true God. He entered our history; he shared our journey. He came to free us from darkness and to grant us light. In him was revealed the grace, the mercy, and the tender love of the Father. Jesus is Love incarnate. He is not simply a teacher of wisdom or an ideal for which we strive, knowing all the while that we will always fall short. Jesus is the meaning of life and history, who has pitched his tent in our midst.

16

Transformed by Love

The Savior is able to transform our lives with his grace, with the power of the Holy Spirit, and with the power of love. The Holy Spirit infuses our hearts with God's love, an inexhaustible source of purification, new life, and freedom. The Virgin Mary fully lived this reality, allowing herself to be "baptized" by the Holy Spirit who inundated her with his power. May she, who prepared for the coming of Christ with the totality of her existence, help us follow her example and guide our steps to the Lord.

17

God's Greatest Gesture of Love

The grace of God appears in Jesus, to whom the Virgin Mary gave birth in the manner that every child enters this world. But he came not "from the earth" but "from heaven," from God. In this way, with the incarnation of the Son, God opened the way to a new life founded not on selfishness but on love. Jesus' birth is our Heavenly Father's greatest gesture of love.

From this we derive our hope as Christians, that in our poverty we may know that we are loved, that we have been visited, that we are accompanied by God, and that we may look upon the world, and on history, as a place in which we walk together with him toward a new heaven and a new earth.

18

Compassionate Love

Jesus arrives with his disciples in Nain, a village in Galilee, right at the moment when a funeral is taking place. A boy, the only son of a widow, is being carried for burial. Jesus immediately fixes his gaze on the crying mother. The Evangelist Luke says, "And when the Lord saw her, he had compassion on her" (Luke 7:13). This "compassion" is God's love for humanity. It is mercy—the attitude of God in contact with human misery, with our destitution, suffering, and anguish. The biblical term *compassion* recalls a mother's womb. The mother in fact reacts in a way all her own when confronting the pain of her children. It is in this way, according to Scripture, that God loves us. What is the fruit of this love and mercy? It is life!

19

God's Merciful Love

The word *mercy* (*misericordia*) is composed of two words: *misery* (*miseria*) and *heart* (*cuore*). The word *heart* symbolizes the ability to love, and the word *mercy* represents love that reaches out and embraces the misery of the human person. It is love that takes on our suffering as its own, with a desire to free us from it. "The Word became flesh" with the intention of sharing in all our frailties and experiencing our human condition, even taking up the Cross, with all the pain of human existence. Such is the depth of God's compassion and mercy: self-destruction in order to become a companion at the service of our wounded humanity.

20

Love Multiplies

Through Jesus Christ, God calls us to imitate his own way of loving: "As I have loved you, that you also love one another" (John 13:34). To the extent to which Christians live this love, they become authentic disciples of Christ to the world. Love cannot bear being locked up in itself. By its nature it is open, it spreads and bears fruit, and it always kindles new love.

21
Love as God Loves

Being Christian does not mainly mean belonging to a certain culture or adhering to a certain doctrine. Being Christian means joining one's own life, in all its aspects, to the person of Jesus and, through him, to the Father. For this purpose, Jesus promises the outpouring of the Holy Spirit to his disciples. And because of the Holy Spirit and the Love that unites the Father and the Son and proceeds from them, we may all live the very life of Jesus. The Spirit, in fact, teaches us the single most indispensable thing: to love as God loves.

22

Love Is Greater Than Our Differences

The Word of God calls us to love one another, even if we do not always understand one another or get along. For it is in our contrasts that Christian love is seen—a love that manifests despite differences of opinion or character. Love is greater than these differences! This is the love that Jesus taught us. It is a redeeming love, free from selfishness. It is a love that gives our hearts joy, as Jesus himself said: "These things I have spoken to you, that my joy may be in you, and that your joy may be full" (John 15:11).

23

We Are All Included in God's Love

Inclusion, an act of mercy, is manifested in opening one's arms wide to welcome without excluding or labeling others according to their social status, language, race, culture, or religion. The person we find at work or in our neighborhood is a person to love as God loves. Some might say, "But he is from that country or that country, or of this religion or that religion. . . ." In the end, he is a person whom God loves, and I must love him. This is what it means to include. This is inclusion.

Jesus' arms open wide on the cross show that no one is excluded from his love and his mercy—not even the greatest sinner. No one!

24
Inexhaustible Love

Good Friday is the culminating moment of love. The death of Jesus, who on the Cross surrenders himself to the Father in order to offer salvation to the entire world, expresses love given to the end, a love without end. A love that seeks to embrace everyone, that excludes no one. A love that extends over time and space: an inexhaustible source of salvation to which each of us, sinners, can draw. If God has shown us his supreme love in the death of Jesus, then we, too, regenerated by the Holy Spirit, can and must love one another.

25

Loving Those Who Oppose Us

It is impossible to measure the love of God. God's love is without measure! And so we become capable of loving even those who do not love us—and this is not easy. Because if we know that a person doesn't like us, then we also tend to bear ill will. But no, we must love that person. [We must oppose] evil with good, with pardon, with sharing, and with welcome. Thanks to Jesus and to his Spirit, even our lives become "bread broken" for our brothers.

In living like this, we discover true joy! The joy of making of oneself a gift, of reciprocating the great gift we have first received without merit of our own. This is what it means to imitate Jesus. Don't forget these two things: The measure of the love of God is love without measure. And, following Jesus, we, with the Eucharist, make our lives a gift.

26

Love Is the Mark of a Christian

Love is the concrete sign that demonstrates faith in God the Father, Son, and Holy Spirit. Love is the badge of the Christian, as Jesus told us: "By this all men will know that you are my disciples, if you have love for one another" (John 13:35). It's a contradiction for Christians to hate. The devil always seeks to make us hate because he's a troublemaker; he doesn't know love. And God is love!

27

Love Inspires Evangelization

The primary reason for evangelizing is our love for Jesus, which we have received, as well as the experience of salvation, which urges us to love him more and more. What kind of love would not feel the need to speak of the beloved, to point him out, to make him known? If we do not feel an intense desire to share this love, we need to pray insistently that [Jesus] will once more touch our hearts. We need to implore his grace daily, asking him to open our cold hearts and shake up our lukewarm and superficial lives.

28

Love Spurs Conversion

Jesus persuaded people with his kindness. Through his love and his way of being, he touched the depths of people's hearts, and they felt attracted to God's love and compelled to change their lifestyles. For example, the conversion of Matthew (Matthew 9:9–13) and of Zacchaeus (Luke 19:1–10) happened in exactly this manner, because they felt loved by Jesus and, through him, by the Father. True conversion happens when we accept the gift of grace. And we will know this conversion is authentic when we become aware of the needs of our brothers and are ready to draw near to them.

29

Love Is Found in Humble Service

When Jesus gives us a grace, forgives us our sins, embraces us, and loves us, he does not do so halfway but completely. Jesus fills our hearts and our lives with his love, with his forgiveness, with his compassion. Thus, Jesus models to his disciples how to carry out his command and follow his path: feed the people and keep them united, being at the service of life and of communion.

Love, therefore, is the practical service that we offer to others. Love is not a word, it is a deed, a service—a *humble* service, *hidden* and *silent*, as Jesus said: "Do not let your left hand know what your right hand is doing" (Matthew 6:3). Humble service entails putting the gifts that the Holy Spirit has given us at others' disposal so that the community might thrive (1 Corinthians 12:4–11). Furthermore, humble service is expressed in the sharing of material goods, so that no one will be left in need. This sharing with and dedication to those in need is the lifestyle that God suggests, even to non-Christians, as the authentic path of humanity.

30

The Anointing Love of the Holy Spirit

The Holy Spirit anoints. He anointed Jesus inwardly, and he anoints his disciples so that they can have the mind of Christ and be disposed to lives of peace and communion. Through the anointing of the Spirit, our human nature is sealed with the holiness of Jesus Christ, and we are enabled to love our brothers and sisters with the same love God has for us.

31

Service Spreads the Practice of Love

I am grateful for the soup kitchens in which many volunteers offer their services, giving food to people who are alone, in need, unemployed, or homeless. These soup kitchens and other works of mercy—such as visiting the sick and the imprisoned—are a training ground for charity that spreads the culture of giving, as those who work in these places are motivated by God's love and by the wisdom of the Gospel. In this way, serving others becomes a testimony of love, which makes the love of Christ visible and credible.

32

Love without End

The first sign of love "without end" (John 13:1) is when Jesus washes the disciples' feet. "The Lord and Master" (John 13:14) stoops to his disciples' feet, as only servants would have done. Jesus shows us by example that we need to allow his love to reach us, to lower itself to us. For we cannot love without first letting ourselves be loved by him, without experiencing his surprising tenderness, without accepting that true love consists of concrete service.

33

Small Acts of Love

There are many small and great actions that obey the Lord's commandment, "Love one another as I have loved you" (John 15:12). Small everyday actions of compassion—to an elderly person, a child, a sick person, a lonely person, those in difficulty, those without a home, those without work, an immigrant, or a refugee—manifest the love that Christ taught us. Thanks to the strength of the Word of Christ, each of us can become the brother or sister to those we encounter.

34

The Greatest Commandment

Love for God and neighbor is the greatest commandment of the Gospel. The Lord calls us to respond generously to the Gospel's call to love, placing God at the center of our lives and dedicating ourselves to the service of our brothers and sisters, especially those most in need of support and consolation.

35

The Symbol of Serving with Love

On Holy Thursday, Jesus institutes the Eucharist, anticipating his sacrifice on Golgotha. To make the Apostles understand the love that enlivens him, Jesus washes their feet and offers once again the example of how they must act. The Eucharist is the love that becomes service. It is the sublime presence of Christ who wishes to relieve hunger from every man and woman, especially the weakest, to enable them to undertake a journey of witnessing amid the difficulties of the world.

36

Embodying God's Tender Love

The Lord tells us, "By this everyone will know that you are my disciples, if you have love for one another" (John 13:35). Faith opens us to a love that is concrete—a practical, generous, and compassionate love that can build and rebuild hope when all seems lost. In this way, we share in God's own work, which the apostle John describes in showing us a God who wipes the tears of his children. God carries out this divine work with the same tender love that a mother has when she dries the tears of her children. What a beautiful question the Lord can ask us at the end of the day: How many tears did you dry today?

37

Serving the Beloved Suffering

Jesus says, "Truly I tell you that, just as you did it to one of the least of these my brothers, you did it to me" (Matthew 25:40). These least of our brethren, whom he loves dearly, are the hungry and the sick, the stranger and the prisoner, the poor and the abandoned, the suffering who receive no help, and the needy who are cast aside. On their faces we can imagine Jesus' own face; on their lips, even if pursed in pain, we can hear his words, "This is my body" (Matthew 26:26).

38

Investing in Love

Jesus knocks on the doors of our hearts through the poor, who are thirsting for our love. When we overcome our indifference and, in the name of Jesus, give ourselves to the least of his brethren, we are his good and faithful friends, with whom he loves to dwell.

. . . Drawing near to the poor in our midst will touch our lives. It will remind us of what really counts: loving God and our neighbor. Only this lasts forever—everything else fades away. What we invest in love will remain; the rest vanishes.

39

Gaining Earth or Heaven?

Today we might ask ourselves, *What matters to me in life? Where am I investing? In fleeting riches, with which we're never satisfied, or in the wealth bestowed by God, who gives eternal life?* This is the choice before us: to live in order to gain things on earth or to give things away in order to gain heaven. Where heaven is concerned, what matters is not what we have but what we give, for "those who store up treasures for themselves do not grow rich in the sight of God" (Luke 12:21).

40

Love That Does Not Perish

The Eucharist communicates the Lord's love for us—a love so great that it nourishes us with himself. This is a love freely given, available to every person who hungers and needs to regenerate his strength. To live the experience of faith means to allow oneself to be nourished by the Lord and to build one's existence not with material goods but with the reality that does not perish: the gifts of God, his Word and his Body.

41

The Secret of Love

There is always a temptation to be overcome by a desire to "have to have" what we find pleasing. This is selfishness. Our consumerist culture reinforces this tendency. When we hold too tightly to something, it fades, it dies, and then we're left confused and empty. If you listen to his voice, the Lord will reveal to you the secret of love: caring for others, respecting them, protecting them, and waiting for them. The secret of love is putting tenderness and love into action.

42

The Commandments of Love

In a word, love means fulfilling the last two commandments of God's Law: "You shall not covet your neighbor's house; you shall not covet your neighbor's wife, or his manservant, or his maidservant, or his ox, or his donkey, or anything that is your neighbor's" (Exodus 20:17). Love inspires a sincere esteem for every human being and the recognition of his or her own right to happiness. It means loving a person and seeing him or her with the eyes of God, who gives us everything "for our enjoyment" (1 Timothy 6:17).

As a result of this love, we will feel a deep sense of happiness and peace. This same deeply rooted love also leads us to reject the injustice of some [people] possessing too much and others too little. It moves us to find ways to help society's outcasts find a modicum of joy. And that is not envy but the desire for equality.

43

Love Has No Price

Do not be content with mediocrity, with "simply going with the flow" and being comfortable and laid-back. Don't believe those who distract you from the real treasure—which you are—by telling you that life is beautiful only if you have many possessions. Be skeptical of those who try to make you believe you're important only if you act tough like the heroes in films or if you wear the latest fashions. Your happiness has no price. It cannot be bought. It is not an app that you can download or an update that will bring you freedom and grandeur in love. True freedom is something else altogether.

44

Love Is Free

Dear young friends, at this stage in your lives, you have a growing desire to demonstrate and receive affection. The Lord, if you let him teach you, will show you how to make tenderness and affection even more beautiful. He will guide your hearts to "love without being possessive," to love others without trying to own them but by letting them be free. Because love is free! There is no true love that is not free. The freedom that the Lord gives us is his love for us. He is always close to each one of us.

45

Love Is Not Earned

None of us can live without love. Many of us fall prey to believing that this love must be earned. Perhaps a good part of our anguish comes from believing that if we are not strong, attractive, and beautiful, no one will take care of us. Many seek visibility only to fill an interior void, as if always needing approval.

However, can you imagine a world in which everyone is looking for ways to attract the attention of others, and no one is willing to give love freely to another person? A world without freely given love! It appears to be a human world, but in reality it's hellish. Much of humanity's narcissism conceals a feeling of loneliness and isolation. And behind this behavior lies a question: *Is it possible that I do not deserve to be loved?*

In Jesus Christ, we are all wanted, we are all loved, we are all desired.

46

Our Hunger for Love

Besides physical hunger, we experience another hunger, a hunger that cannot be satiated with ordinary food. It's a hunger for life, a hunger for love, a hunger for eternity. And the sign of *manna*—like the entire experience of Exodus—also contains this hunger: it was the symbol of a food that satisfied a deep human need. Jesus gives us this food, or rather, *he himself* is the living bread that gives life to the world (John 6:51). His Body is the true food in the form of bread; his Blood is the true drink in the form of wine. These aren't simple nourishments to satisfy the body, like manna. The Body of Christ is the bread for the end of times, capable of giving life—eternal life—because this bread is made of love.

47

Love for the Prodigal Son

The greater the sin, the greater the love that must be shown by the Church to those who repent. With how much love Jesus looks at us! With how much love he heals our sinful hearts! Our sins never scare him. Let us consider the prodigal son who, upon returning to his father, considers making a speech, but his father won't let him speak. Instead, his father embraces him (Luke 15:17–24). This is how Jesus is with us. "Father, I have so many sins. . . ." But he will be glad if you go [to him]—he will embrace you with such love! Don't be afraid.

48

Friendship and Love

At the Last Supper, Jesus says, "This is my commandment, that you love one another as I have loved you" (John 15:12). Thinking of his imminent sacrifice on the cross, he adds, "Greater love has no man than this, that a man lay down his life for his friends. You are my friends, if you do what I command you" (vv. 13–14). These words summarize Jesus' message and, actually, all that he did: Jesus gave his life for his friends. Friends who did not understand him, friends who abandoned, betrayed, and denied him at the crucial moment. His message tells us that he loves us, even though we don't deserve his love. Jesus loves us in this same way!

49

Stealing Jesus' Love

Jesus is on the Cross to be with those who are guilty. Through this closeness, he offers them salvation. What was a scandal to the leaders and the first thief and to those who were there and mocked Jesus ended up being the foundation of the good thief's faith. The thief became a witness to Grace when the unthinkable happened to him: *God loved me so much that he died on the Cross for me.* His very faith is a fruit of Christ's grace. It is true, he was a thief, he was a crook, he had stolen things throughout his life. But in the end, he regretted what he had done, and, seeing Jesus, so good and merciful, he managed to *steal* heaven. He is a great thief, this man!

50

Infinite Love

Jesus, even at the height of his suffering, reveals the true face of God, which *is* mercy. Jesus forgives those who are crucifying him, he opens the gates of paradise to the repentant thief, and he touches the heart of the centurion. If the mystery of evil is immeasurable, then the reality of Love poured out through Jesus is infinite, reaching even to the tomb and to hell. Jesus takes on all our pain so that he may redeem it, bringing light to darkness, life to death, love to hatred.

51

Jesus' Burning Gaze of Love

When we stand before Jesus crucified, we see the depth of his love, which exalts and sustains us. But at the same time, unless we are blind, we begin to realize that Jesus' gaze, burning with love, expands to embrace all his people. We realize once more that he wants to make use of us to draw closer to his beloved people. He takes us from the midst of his people, and he sends us to his people; without this sense of belonging we cannot understand our deepest identity.

52

Mary's Look of Love

From the Cross, Jesus looks at his Mother and entrusts her to the apostle John, saying, "This is your son." We are all present in John . . . and Jesus' look of love entrusts us to the maternal care of the Mother. Mary would have remembered another look of love when she was a girl: the gaze of God the Father, who looked upon her humility, her littleness. Mary teaches us that God does not abandon us—he can do great things even with our weaknesses. Let us trust in him. Let us knock at the door of his heart!

53
Silent Love

On Holy Saturday, God is silent, but out of love. On this day, love—silent love—becomes the expectation of life in the Resurrection. It will do us good to consider the silence of Our Lady, "the Believer," who awaited the Resurrection in silence. Our Lady will be the icon of Holy Saturday for us. Think hard about how Our Lady lived that Holy Saturday in expectation. It is love that does not doubt and that hopes in the word of the Lord, that it may be made manifest and resplendent on the day of Easter.

54

Mary Is a Source of True Love

Our pilgrimage of faith has been inseparably linked to Mary ever since Jesus, dying on the Cross, gave her to us as our Mother, saying: "Behold your Mother!" (John 19:27). From that moment on, the Mother of God also became our Mother! When the faith of the disciples was most tested by difficulties and uncertainties, Jesus entrusted them to Mary, who was the first to believe and whose faith would never fail. Mary became our Mother when she lost her divine Son. Her sorrowful heart was enlarged to make room for all men and women, whether good or bad, and she loves them as she loved Jesus.

The woman at the wedding at Cana in Galilee who gave her faith-filled cooperation so that the wonders of God could be displayed, the woman at Calvary who kept alive the flame of faith in the resurrection of her Son, offers her love to each and every person. Mary becomes a source of hope and true joy for us!

55

Jesus Died for Love

Jesus does not passively experience the love that leads to his sacrifice, nor does he consider his sacrifice a fatal destiny. He does not, of course, conceal his deep human distress as he faces a violent death, but with absolute trust, he commends himself to the Father. Jesus gave himself up to death voluntarily to reciprocate the love of God the Father, in perfect union with his will, and to demonstrate his love for us. On the Cross, Jesus "loved me and gave himself for me" (Galatians 2:20). Each of us can say, "He loved me and gave himself for me." Each one of us can say "for me."

56

The Way of True Love Is Sacrifice

Jesus on the Cross feels the whole weight of evil, and with the force of God's love, he conquers it. He defeats it with his resurrection. This is the good that Jesus does for us on the throne of the Cross. Christ's Cross embraced with love never leads to sadness but to joy—joy in having been saved and in doing a little of what Jesus did on the day of his death.

The temptation is to want to follow a Christ without the cross. But Jesus reminds us that his way is the way of love, and that there is no true love without self-sacrifice. We are called not to let ourselves be absorbed by the vision of this world but to be ever more aware of the need and of the effort for us Christians to walk against the current and uphill.

57

Love on the Cross

For a Christian, speaking about power and strength means referring to the power of the Cross and the strength of Jesus' love—a love that remains steadfast and whole, even when facing rejection. A love that is shown in the total surrender of oneself for the benefit of humanity.

Those who look at the Cross cannot help but see the astonishing generosity of love. One could say, "Father, that was a failure!" But it is precisely in the failure of sin, in the failure of human ambitions, that the triumph of the Cross is there, the generosity of love is there. In the failure of the Cross, we see love, a love that is gratuitous, which Jesus gives us.

58

God's Love Is Abundant

If we look at the history of salvation, we see that the whole of God's revelation is an unceasing and untiring love for us. God is like a father or mother who loves with an unconditional love and pours it out abundantly on every creature. Jesus' death on the Cross is the culmination of the love story between God and humanity—a love so great that God alone can understand it.

59

Christ's Love Always Triumphs

The history of sin can be understood only in the light of God's love and forgiveness. Were sin the only thing that mattered, we would be the most desperate of creatures. But the promised triumph of Christ's love enfolds everyone in the Father's mercy. The word of God leaves no doubt about this. The Immaculate Virgin stands before us as a privileged witness of this promise and its fulfilment.

60

The Living Sign of God's Love

In our fragmented lives, the Lord comes to meet us with a loving "fragility" in the Eucharist. The Eucharist is the memorial of God's love. There, "[Christ's] sufferings are remembered" (*II Vespers, antiphon for the Magnificat*) and we recall God's love for us, which gives us strength and support on our journey. This is why the Eucharistic commemoration does us so much good: it is not an abstract, cold, and superficial memory but a living remembrance that comforts us with God's love. A memory that is both recollection and imitation.

The Eucharist gives us the encouragement that, even on the roughest road, we are not alone. The Lord does not forget us. Whenever we turn to him, he restores us with his love.

61
The Supreme Act of Love

Christ is the fullness of life, and when he faced death, he destroyed it forever. Christ's Passover is the definitive victory over death because he transformed his death in the supreme act of love. He died out of love! And in the Eucharist he wishes to communicate to us his paschal, victorious love. If we receive him with faith, we too can truly love God and neighbor. We can love as he loved us, by giving our lives.

If Christ's love is within us, then we can give ourselves fully to others, knowing that, even if someone were to wound us, we would not die. The martyrs gave their own lives in this certainty of Christ's victory over death. Only if we experience this power of Christ—the power of his love—are we truly free to give ourselves without fear.

62

Losing Our Lives for Love

Jesus teaches that it is only when we lose our lives for love of him that we truly save them (Luke 9:24). This was the revolution experienced by Paul, but it is, and always has been, the Christian revolution. We live no longer for ourselves, for our own interests and "image," but in the image of Christ, *for* him and *following* him, *with* his love and *in* his love.

63

Surrendering to the Goodness of Love

The gift of "fear of the Lord" does not mean being afraid of God. We know well that God is Father, that he loves us and wants our salvation and that he always forgives, always. Thus, there is no reason to be scared of him. Fear of the Lord, instead, is the gift of the Holy Spirit through whom we are reminded of how small we are before God and his love, and that our good lies in humble, respectful, and trusting self-abandonment into his hands. This is fear of the Lord: abandonment in the goodness of our Father who loves us so much.

64

Surrendering to the Promise of Love

Grounded in love, a man and a woman can promise each other mutual love in a gesture that engages their entire lives and mirrors their faith. Promising love forever is possible when we perceive a plan bigger than our own ideas and undertakings, a plan that sustains us and enables us to surrender our future entirely to the one we love.

65

Loving beyond Ourselves

The sacrament of marriage is a great act of faith and love. It takes courage to believe in the beauty of the creative act of God and to live that love that is always urging us to go on, beyond ourselves and even beyond our own family. The Christian vocation to love unconditionally and without limit is, by the grace of Christ, at the foundation of marriage.

66

Love Is Grounded in Truth

Genuine love ultimately requires truth, and the shared contemplation of the truth that is Jesus Christ enables love to become deep and enduring.

Only to the extent that love is grounded in truth can it endure over time, transcend the passing moment, and be sufficiently solid to sustain a shared journey. If love is not tied to truth, it falls prey to fickle emotions and cannot stand the test of time.

67

Love and Truth Are Inseparable

If love needs truth, then truth also needs love. Love and truth are inseparable. Without love, truth becomes cold, impersonal, and oppressive for people's day-to-day lives. The truth we seek, the truth that gives meaning to our journey through life, enlightens us whenever we are touched by love. One who loves realizes that love is an experience of truth and that it opens our eyes to see reality in a new way, in union with the beloved.

68

Marriage Mirrors God's Love

When a man and woman celebrate the Sacrament of Matrimony, God is mirrored in them. God impresses upon them his own features and the indelible character of his love. Marriage is the icon of God's love for us. Indeed, God mirrors communion too: the three Persons of the Father, the Son, and the Holy Spirit live eternally in perfect unity. And this is precisely the mystery of Matrimony: God makes of the two spouses one single life.

69

When Love Is Worn Out

The love of Christ, which has blessed and sanctified the union of husband and wife, is able to sustain a couple's love and renew it when it becomes lost, wounded, or worn out. The love of Christ can restore their joy of journeying together. This is what marriage is all about: man and woman walking together, wherein the husband helps his wife become ever more a woman, and the woman helps her husband become ever more a man. This is the task they both share.

70

The Gift of Love in Matrimony

Love has been poured into our hearts through the Holy Spirit (Romans 5:5). This is also the love that is given to spouses in the Sacrament of Marriage. It is love that nourishes their relationship through joy and pain, through untroubled and difficult moments. It is love that gives rise to the desire to bear children, await them, welcome them, raise them, and teach them. It is the same love that Jesus shows toward children: "Let the children come to me, do not hinder them; for to such belongs the kingdom of God" (Mark 10:14).

71

Sealed with God's Love

Children are loved before having done anything to deserve it, before knowing how to talk or think, even before coming into the world! Being a child is the basic condition for knowing the love of God, which is the ultimate source of this authentic miracle. In the soul of every child, although it may be vulnerable, God places the seal of this love, which is the basis of the child's personal dignity—a dignity that nothing, and no one, can ever destroy.

72

The Promise of Love to Every Child

I like it very much when I see fathers and mothers bringing me a baby boy or girl, and I ask, "How old is he or she?" And they say, "Three weeks, four weeks," and, "I ask for the Lord's blessing." This, too, is called love. Love is the promise that a man and woman make to every child from the moment he or she is conceived in their minds. Children come into the world and they expect this promise of love to be confirmed. They expect it in a complete, trusting, and defenseless way.

73
Families Growing in Love

The word of God tells us that the family is entrusted to a man, a woman, and their children, so that they may become a communion of persons in the image of the union of the Father, the Son, and the Holy Spirit. Begetting and raising children, for its part, mirrors God's creative work. The family is called to join in daily prayer, read the word of God, and share in Eucharistic communion, thus growing in love and becoming ever more fully a temple in which the Spirit dwells.

74

Love Powers the Family

What is the power that unites a family? Love. And the One who sows love in our hearts is God. It is precisely God's love that gives meaning to our small daily tasks and helps us face great trials. This is the true treasure of humankind: going forward in life with love, a love that the Lord has sown in our hearts. The Lord's love is our true treasure.

75

Love in Our Families

At the foundation of everything is love, love that God gives us that "is not arrogant or rude. Love does not insist on its own way; it is not irritable or resentful; it does not rejoice at wrong, but . . . bears all things, believes all things, hopes all things, endures all things" (1 Corinthians 13:5–7). Even the best families need support, and it takes a lot of patience to support one another. But such is life. Life is not lived in a laboratory but in reality.

76

We Must Learn How to Love Every Day

Knowing how to love is never something acquired once and for all. We must begin anew every day. We must practice it so that our love for the brothers and sisters we encounter may become mature and free from limitations or sins that render it incomplete, egotistical, sterile, or unfaithful. Listen to this: we must patiently follow the school of Christ every day. We must forgive and look to Jesus with the help of our "advocate," the Holy Spirit. We must learn the art of loving every day.

77
Love Helps Us Up

God created us to be on our feet. There is a lovely song that mountain climbers sing as they climb that goes, "In climbing, the important thing is not to not fall but to not remain fallen!" In life, we must have the courage to pick ourselves up and allow ourselves to be raised up by Jesus. His hand is often given through the hand of a friend, of one's parents, of those who accompany us throughout life. Jesus himself is present in them. So, arise! God wants us up on our feet!

78

Service Is the Sign of True Love

Service is the sign of true love. Those who love know how to serve others. We learn this especially in our families, where we become servants out of love for one another. In the heart of the family, no one is rejected. Everyone has the same value. I remember my mother was once asked which of her five children (we are five brothers) she loved the most. And she said, "It is like the fingers on my hand: if I prick one of them, it is as if the others are pricked too." In the family, children are loved as they are. No one is rejected.

79

Harmonious Love in Families

God alone knows how to create harmony from differences. But if there is not enough of God's love [in our relationships], a family loses its harmony. Self-centeredness prevails and joy fades. The family that experiences the joy of faith communicates it naturally, and that family is the salt of the earth and the light of the world. They are the leaven of society as a whole.

80
Love Unites

These days, it's easy to imagine a group of people united in a common cause, sharing the same destiny and a single purpose. But we find it harder to imagine a unity in one truth. We tend to think that a unity of this sort is incompatible with freedom of thought and personal autonomy. Yet the experience of love shows us that a common vision is possible, for through love we learn how to see reality through the eyes of others, not as something that impoverishes our vision but enriches it.

81

Listening Is Love

We devote periods of quiet time only to the things or the people we love. God, whom we love, wishes to speak to us. Because of this love, we can take as much time as we need, like every true disciple: "Speak, Lord, for your servant is listening" (1 Samuel 3:9).

82

Families Illuminate God's Love

By their witness as well as their words, families speak to others about Jesus. They pass on the faith, they inspire a desire for God, and they reflect the beauty of the Gospel and its way of life. Christian marriages thus enliven society by their witness of fraternity, their social concern, their outspokenness on behalf of the underprivileged, their luminous faith, and their active hope. Their fruitfulness expands and makes God's love present in society in countless ways.

83

The Love of Families in Cities

The lack of love and smiles has turned our cities into deserts. So much entertainment, so many things for wasting time and making people laugh, but love is lacking. The smile of a family can overcome this erosion of our cities. This is the victory of family love. No economic and political engineering can substitute for this contribution of families. The Babel project builds lifeless skyscrapers. The Spirit of God instead makes the desert fruitful (Isaiah 32:15). We must come out of the towers and from the armored vaults of the elite to spend time in the homes and open spaces of the multitudes, open to the love of families.

84

Creation as a Gift of Love

The Bible speaks of all creation as a beautiful work of God's love. The Book of Genesis says that "God saw everything that he had made, and behold, it was very good" (Genesis 1:31). Only when it is finished does God "rest." We understand from this image that God's love, which brought forth the world, was not an impromptu decision. No. It was a beautiful work. The love of God created the concrete conditions for an irrevocable covenant, one that is strong and lasting.

85

Love for the Planet

An authentic faith always involves a deep desire to change the world, to transmit values, and to leave this earth somehow better than we found it. We love this magnificent planet on which God put us, and we love the human family that dwells here, with all its tragedies and struggles, its hopes and aspirations, its strengths and weaknesses.

86

Every Human Life Was Formed in Love

The Creator says to each of us, "Before I formed you in the womb, I knew you" (Jeremiah 1:5). We were conceived in the heart of God, and for this reason, "each of us is the result of a thought of God. Each of us is willed, each of us is loved, each of us is necessary" (Pope Benedict XVI, April 24, 2005). How wonderful is the certainty that each human life is not adrift in the midst of hopeless chaos, in a world ruled by pure chance or endlessly recurring cycles.

87

Our Destiny Is Love

Our truest destiny and our deepest vocation is to be loved, to be transformed by love, to be transformed by the beauty of God. Let us look to our Mother and allow her to look upon us, for she loves us so much. Let us allow ourselves to be watched over by her so that we may learn how to be more humble and courageous in following the Word of God and that we may learn how to welcome the tender embrace of her Son, Jesus, an embrace that gives us life, hope, and peace.

88

The Vocation of Love

Faith is no refuge for the fainthearted but something that enhances our lives. Faith makes us aware of a magnificent calling: the vocation of love. It assures us that this love is trustworthy and worth embracing, for it is based on God's faithfulness, which is stronger than our every weakness. When we allow ourselves to be guided by this love, the horizons of our lives will broaden, and we will receive a firm hope that will not disappoint.

89

The Light of Love

Christian faith, inasmuch as it proclaims the truth of God's total love and opens us to the power of that love, penetrates to the core of our human experience. Each of us comes to the light because of love, and each of us is called to love in order to remain in the light.

90

Love Bears Fruit

Jesus says, "On these two commandments depend all the law and the prophets" (Matthew 22:40). [The commandments to love God and neighbor] are the most important, and the others depend on these two. Jesus lived his life precisely in this way: preaching and practicing what truly matters and is essential—namely, love. Love gives feeling and fruitfulness to life and to the journey of life: without love, both life and faith remain sterile.

91

Our Love Story with God

What is at the foundation of our faith? An act of mercy by which Jesus binds us to him. And the Christian life is our response to this love. It is like the history of two people in love: God and humanity meet, seek, find, celebrate, and love each other, just like the lovers in the Song of Songs. Everything else comes as a result of this relationship. The Church is the family of Jesus into which he pours his love. It is this love that the Church safeguards and desires to give to all.

92

The Lord's Love Waits for You

The Church's joy is to mirror the light of Christ. The Church is made up of the people who have experienced this attraction and bear it within, in their hearts and in their lives. I would like to say—sincerely—to those who feel far from God and from the Church, and to all those who are fearful or indifferent: The Lord is also calling you to be a part of his people, and he does so with deep respect and love! The Lord is calling you. The Lord is seeking you. The Lord is waiting for you. The Lord does not proselytize; he loves, and this love seeks you, waits for you—you who at this moment do not believe or are far away. This is the unconditional love of God.

93

Jesus' Love Is Limitless

Out of love, Christ became human. Out of love, Christ died and rose again. And out of love, Christ is always at our side, in the beautiful moments and in the difficult ones. Jesus loves us always—until the end—without limit and without measure. He loves us all, to the point that each of us can say, "He gave his life for me." For me! Jesus' faithfulness does not fail, even in the face of our infidelity. St. Paul reminds us of this. He writes, "If we are faithless, he remains faithful, for he cannot deny himself" (2 Timothy 2:13).

94
God's Love Never Gives Up

The heart of the Good Shepherd not only shows us mercy but is itself mercy. There the Father's love shines forth. There we know we are welcomed and understood as we are, with all our sins and limitations. There we know with certainty that we are chosen and loved.

The heart of the Good Shepherd also tells us that his love is limitless: it is never exhausted, and it never gives up. There we see God's infinite and boundless self-giving, we find the source of faithful and humble love that sets us free, and we constantly discover anew that Jesus loves us "even to the end" (John 13:1)—to the very end, without ever imposing.

95

Jesus Returns Our Loved Ones to Us

Jesus brought the only son of a widow back to life and "gave him back to his mother" (Luke 7:11–15). This is our hope! The Lord will bring back all our loved ones who are gone, and we will be together with them. This hope does not disappoint.

In this faith, we can console one another, knowing that the Lord has conquered death once and for all. Our loved ones are not lost in the darkness of nothing; hope assures us that they are in the good and strong hands of God. Love is stronger than death.

96

Praying for Our Loved Ones

Praying for the dead is, first and foremost, a sign of appreciation for the witness they have left us and for the good they have done. Our prayers thank the Lord for having given them to us and for their love and friendship. The Church prays for the deceased in a particular way during Holy Mass. The priest states, "Be mindful, O Lord, of thy servants who are gone before us with the sign of faith, and rest in sleep of peace. To these, O Lord, and to all that sleep in Christ, grant we beseech thee a place of refreshment, light and peace" (Roman Canon). It is a simple, effective, and meaningful remembrance, because it entrusts our loved ones to God's mercy.

We pray with Christian hope that they may be with him in Paradise as we wait to be reunited. As Jesus promised, we will all rise again, and we will all be forever with him.

97

Love Will Buoy Us beyond Death

Let love grow, make it stronger, and it will guard you until the day that every tear shall be wiped away, when "death shall be no more, neither shall there be mourning nor crying nor pain any more" (Revelation 21:4). If we allow ourselves to be sustained by this faith, then the experience of grief can generate even stronger family bonds as well as a new openness to the pain of other families, a new brotherhood with families that is born, and reborn, in hope.

98

Jesus' Gaze of Love

Always remember this: life is a journey. Life is a journey to meet Jesus at the end and then forever. A journey in which we do not encounter Jesus is not a Christian journey. It is for the Christian to continually encounter Jesus, to watch him, and to let himself be watched over by Jesus because Jesus watches us with love. He loves us so much and is always watching over us.

99

Christ's Death Paved the Way for Love

Jesus' reign is truly not of this world (John 18:36). For the grandeur of his kingdom is not power as defined by this world but the love of God, a love capable of encountering and healing all things. Christ humbled himself to us out of this love. He lived our human misery; he suffered the lowest point of our human condition: injustice, betrayal, abandonment. He experienced death, the tomb, and hell.

Our King went to the ends of the universe to embrace and save every living being. He did not condemn us, nor did he conquer us, and he never disregarded our freedom. Instead, he paved the way with a humble love that forgives all things, hopes all things, and sustains all things (1 Corinthians 13:7). This love alone overcame and continues to overcome our worst enemies: sin, death, and fear.

100

Jesus Never Tires of Loving

On Holy Thursday, Jesus was with the disciples at the table, celebrating the feast of Passover. The passage describing this scene in John's Gospel contains a phrase that is at the very core of what Jesus did for us: "having loved his own who were in the world, he loved them to the end" (John 13:1). Jesus loved us. *Jesus loves us.* Without limit, always, to the end. He loves us all, to the point of giving his life for each one of us.

His love is like that: personal. Jesus' love never disappoints, because he never tires of loving, just as he never tires of forgiving, never tires of embracing us. Jesus loved us, every one of us, to the end.

Sources

1: Love Is Kindled in Darkness
General Audience, April 1, 2015
www.vatican.va

2: God's Love Never Ends
General Audience, April 26, 2017
www.vatican.va

3: God's Love Waits for Us
General Audience, November 23, 2016
www.vatican.va
Homily, April 7, 2013
www.vatican.va

4: Rock-Solid Love
Homily, June 21, 2015
www.vatican.va

5: Generous Love
General Audience, January 13, 2016
www.vatican.va

6: God's Love Is Tangible
Angelus, May 26, 2013
www.vatican.va

7: God's Love Is Close to Us
Angelus, June 15, 2014
www.vatican.va

8: God's Love Transforms
Homily, June 21, 2015
www.vatican.va

9: The Ultimate Sign of Love
Homily, December 24, 2014
www.vatican.va

10: Love Carries Us through Uncertainty
Homily, December 24, 2017
www.vatican.va

11: The Bread of Love
Homily, December 24, 2016
www.vatican.va

12: Loving the Child Jesus
General Audience, December 30, 2015
www.vatican.va

13: God's Love Is Humble
Homily, January 6, 2015
www.vatican.va

14: God's Power Is Love
Homily, March 21, 2015
www.vatican.va

15: Love Incarnate
Homily, December 24, 2013
www.vatican.va

16: Transformed by Love
Angelus, December 10, 2017
www.vatican.va

17: God's Greatest Gesture of Love
General Audience, December 27, 2017
www.vatican.va
Angelus, January 5, 2014
www.vatican.va

18: Compassionate Love
Angelus, June 9, 2013
www.vatican.va

19: God's Merciful Love
Homily, December 12, 2015
www.vatican.va

20: Love Multiplies
Homily, December 12, 2015
www.vatican.va

21: Love as God Loves
Regina Caeli, May 15, 2016
www.vatican.va

22: Love Is Greater Than Our Differences
Regina Caeli, May 10, 2015
www.vatican.va

23: We Are All Included in God's Love
Jubilee Audience, November 12, 2016
www.vatican.va

24: Inexhaustible Love
General Audience, March 23, 2016
www.vatican.va

25: Loving Those Who Oppose Us
Angelus, June 22, 2014
www.vatican.va

26: Love Is the Mark of a Christian
Angelus, June 15, 2014
www.vatican.va

27: Love Inspires Evangelization
Evangelii Gaudium, 264
www.vatican.va

28: Love Spurs Conversion
Jubilee Audience, June 18, 2016
www.vatican.va

29: Love Is Found in Humble Service
General Audience, August 17, 2016
www.vatican.va
Jubilee Audience, March 12, 2016
www.vatican.va

30: The Anointing Love of the Holy Spirit
Homily, May 24, 2014
www.vatican.va

31: Service Spreads the Practice of Love
Angelus, August 28, 2016
www.vatican.va

32: Love without End
Homily, March 20, 2016
www.vatican.va

33: Small Acts of Love
Regina Caeli, May 10, 2015
www.vatican.va

34: The Greatest Commandment
Regina Caeli, May 21, 2017
www.vatican.va

35: The Symbol of Serving with Love
General Audience, March 23, 2016
www.vatican.va

36: Embodying God's Tender Love
Homily, January 20, 2018
www.vatican.va

37: Serving the Beloved Suffering
Homily, November 19, 2017
www.vatican.va

38: Investing in Love
Homily, November 19, 2017
www.vatican.va

39: Gaining Earth or Heaven?
Homily, November 19, 2017
www.vatican.va

40: Love That Does Not Perish
Homily, June 19, 2014
www.vatican.va

41: The Secret of Love
Homily, April 24, 2016
www.vatican.va

42: The Commandments of Love
Amoris Laetitia, 96
www.vatican.va

43: Love Has No Price
Homily, April 24, 2016
www.vatican.va

44: Love Is Free
Homily, April 24, 2016
www.vatican.va

45: Love Is Not Earned
General Audience, June 14, 2017
www.vatican.va

46: Our Hunger for Love
Homily, June 19, 2014
www.vatican.va

47: Love for the Prodigal Son
Homily, March 13, 2015
www.vatican.va

48: Friendship and Love
Regina Caeli, May 10, 2015
www.vatican.va

49: Stealing Jesus' Love
General Audience, September 28, 2016
www.vatican.va

50: Infinite Love
Homily, March 20, 2016
www.vatican.va

51: Jesus' Burning Gaze of Love
Evangelii Gaudium, 268
www.vatican.va

52: Mary's Look of Love
Homily, September 22, 2013
www.vatican.va

53: Silent Love
General Audience, March 23, 2016
www.vatican.va

54: Mary Is a Source of True Love
Homily, January 1, 2014
www.vatican.va

55: Jesus Died for Love
General Audience, March 27, 2013
www.vatican.va

56: The Way of True Love Is Sacrifice
Homily, March 24, 2013
www.vatican.va
Angelus, September 3, 2017
www.vatican.va

57: Love on the Cross
Angelus, November 22, 2015
www.vatican.va

58: God's Love Is Abundant
General Audience, September 21, 2016
www.vatican.va

59: Christ's Love Always Triumphs
Homily, December 8, 2015
www.vatican.va

60: The Living Sign of God's Love
Homily, June 18, 2017
www.vatican.va

61: The Supreme Act of Love
General Audience, November 22, 2017
www.vatican.va

62: Losing Our Lives for Love
Homily, January 25, 2017
www.vatican.va

63: Surrendering to the Goodness of Love
General Audience, June 11, 2014
www.vatican.va

64: Surrendering to the Promise of Love
Lumen Fidei, 52
www.vatican.va

65: Loving beyond Ourselves
General Audience, May 6, 2015
www.vatican.va

66: Love Is Grounded in Truth
Lumen Fidei, 47
www.vatican.va
Lumen Fidei, 27
www.vatican.va

67: Love and Truth Are Inseparable
Lumen Fidei, 27
www.vatican.va

68: Marriage Mirrors God's Love
General Audience, April 2, 2014
www.vatican.va

69: When Love Is Worn Out
Homily, September 14, 2014
www.vatican.va

70: The Gift of Love in Matrimony
Angelus, October 4, 2015
www.vatican.va

71: Sealed with God's Love
General Audience, February 11, 2015
www.vatican.va

72: The Promise of Love to Every Child
General Audience, October 14, 2015
www.vatican.va

73: Families Growing in Love
Amoris Laetitia, 29
www.vatican.va

74: Love Powers the Family
Angelus, August 11, 2013
www.vatican.va

75: Love in Our Families
General Audience, May 20, 2015
www.vatican.va

76: We Must Learn How to Love Every Day
Regina Caeli, May 21, 2017
www.vatican.va

77: Love Helps Us Up
Homily, April 24, 2016
www.vatican.va

78: Service Is the Sign of True Love
Homily, July 6, 2015
www.vatican.va

79: Harmonious Love in Families
Homily, October 27, 2013
www.vatican.va

80: Love Unites
Lumen Fidei, 47
www.vatican.va

81: Listening Is Love
Evangelii Gaudium, 146
www.vatican.va

82: Families Illuminate God's Love
Amoris Laetitia, 184
www.vatican.va

83: The Love of Families in Cities
General Audience, September 2, 2015
www.vatican.va

84: Creation as a Gift of Love
General Audience, May 27, 2015
www.vatican.va

85: Love for the Planet
Evangelii Gaudium, 183
www.vatican.va

86: Every Human Life Was Formed in Love
Laudato Si, 65
www.vatican.va

87: Our Destiny Is Love
Angelus, December 8, 2013
www.vatican.va

88: The Vocation of Love
Lumen Fidei, 53
www.vatican.va

89: The Light of Love
Lumen Fidei, 32
www.vatican.va

90: Love Bears Fruit
Angelus, October 29, 2017
www.vatican.va

91: Our Love Story with God
General Audience, June 8, 2016
www.vatican.va

92: The Lord's Love Waits for You
Angelus, January 6, 2014
www.vatican.va

93: Jesus' Love Is Limitless
Homily, June 21, 2015
www.vatican.va

94: God's Love Never Gives Up
Homily, June 3, 2016
www.vatican.va

95: Jesus Returns Our Loved Ones to Us
General Audience, June 17, 2015
www.vatican.va

96: Praying for Our Loved Ones
General Audience, November 30, 2016
www.vatican.va

97: Love Will Buoy Us beyond Death
General Audience, June 17, 2015
www.vatican.va

98: Jesus' Gaze of Love
Homily, December 1, 2013
www.vatican.va

99: Christ's Death Paved the Way for Love
Homily, November 20, 2016
www.vatican.va

100: Jesus Never Tires of Loving
Homily, Holy Thursday, April 2, 2015
www.vatican.va